GRAPES, PEACHES AND NECTARINES

As H. R. Tuffin says, 'the successful cultivation of grapes, peaches and nectarines . . . is an art rather than a science'. In this Handbook he deals expertly with all aspects of the cultivation of these delicious fruits and gives advice on the most suitable varieties to grow.

A chapter on the cultivation of grapes outdoors, both for eating purposes and for making wine; has been contributed by Mr R. Barrington Brock of the Viticultural Research Station. He explains the differing methods of pruning necessary to obtain a good crop out of doors in this country.

Mr Tuffin, a professional gardener, is well known for the many prize-winning exhibits of fruit and vegetables he has shown at the Royal Horticultural Society's Halls. He is a member of the Fruit and Vegetable Committee and of the Joint Sweet Pea Committee of the R.H.S.

An Amateur Gardening Handbook

THIS BOOK

IS NO 22 OF THE AMATEUR GARDENING HANDBOOKS

others in the series are

NEW TITLES ARE ADDED FROM TIME TO TIME

AMATEUR GARDENING HANDBOOK NO 22

GRAPES, PEACHES AND NECTARINES

H. R. TUFFIN

WITH A CHAPTER ON *OUTDOOR GRAPES*

BY R. BARRINGTON BROCK

22

W. H. & L. COLLINGRIDGE LTD
2-10 TAVISTOCK STREET COVENT GARDEN LONDON WC2

FIRST PUBLISHED IN 1957

The Amateur Gardening Handbooks
are published by
W. H. & L. Collingridge Limited
2-10 Tavistock Street, London, WC2
and printed and bound in England by
Hazell Watson & Viney Limited
Aylesbury and London

© *W. H. & L. Collingridge Ltd 1957*

CONTENTS

ILLUSTRATIONS

BY CYNTHIA NEWSOME-TAYLOR

FOREWORD

IN the list of choice fruits which we grow in our gardens in this country, the grape, peach and nectarine rank very high. Though they are not now grown to such perfection as they were in the past in large private gardens, I am sure there are many more owners of smaller gardens (in the owner/ driver class) who are ambitious enough to try their hand at growing these delectable fruits, as I am certain there is very much more satisfaction and enjoyment in producing and eating produce from one's own garden than there is in buying from a shop. My own experience of growing these fruits has been in large private gardens, and this book is based on the experience I have thus obtained. The section dealing with the culture of grapes out of doors has been contributed by Mr R. Barrington Brock, of the Viticultural Research Station, Oxted, Surrey.

WARNINGLID,   H. R. TUFFIN
SUSSEX.

7

Part One: Grapes

CHAPTER ONE

ORIGIN AND USES

THE grape-producing vine, *Vitis vinifera*, grows wild in Western Asia, Southern Europe, Algeria and Morocco in North Africa. Birds find the berries very pleasant to eat, and dissemination of seed by this means over ever-increasing areas would have taken place at a very early date. Records of the cultivation of vines go back thousands of years, and we read of vineyards and wine-making in ancient Egypt. The vine in cultivation will grow freely and fruit abundantly in a wide range of temperatures in different parts of the world, including France and Italy, Greece and Turkey, North and South Africa, Australia, America, Spain and Portugal.

In the nourishment of man the grape takes a leading part; it cheers us in health in the form of the many and varied wines made from it, so pleasant to drink, and in sickness it helps to bring the invalid back to health. Grapes play a part in everyday life as a dessert fruit, and when dried they become currants, sultanas and raisins.

CHAPTER TWO

CULTIVATION UNDER GLASS

THE cultivation of the grape in the British Isles is carried out chiefly under the protection of glasshouses (Figs. 1 and 2) either cold or heated by artificial means. Some varieties will grow and ripen their fruit quite satisfactorily in unheated houses, while others will only give of their best regularly every season in a heated house. In hotter summers some of the more difficult ones might be brought successfully to maturity in cold houses, with well-finished berries, but unfortunately our summers are so uncertain. To grow grapes of first-class quality will test the grower to the full, and it is because of this fact that the grape is ranked highest in the classification of fruits in Show Schedules, carrying higher maximum points than any other. The successful cultivation of grapes, peaches and nectarines, and in fact of all the plants grown in gardens by amateur or professional gardeners, is an art rather than a science.

Perhaps it becomes nearer to being an exact science when practised by the large commercial growers, who have to carry out everything to a strict schedule to make their business a successful proposition. Science certainly puts a lot of aids in the way of the small grower, and it is by acquiring a certain amount of knowledge on these matters, and of other certain fundamentals, that success to a greater or lesser degree will be attained. The art will lie in applying the knowledge gained to the best advantage in all the varying conditions which obtain in different gardens. No two gardens are alike, and to be successful in the differing circumstances the grower will need to show adaptability to a marked degree.

PREPARATION OF THE SOIL

To grow grapes on a commercial scale, it will be necessary to choose a suitable situation for the job, where the soil is right and where the natural drainage also is satisfactory. The amateur or private gardener will usually already have a garden and will probably have to improve the existing conditions.

It must be remembered that grape vines will grow to

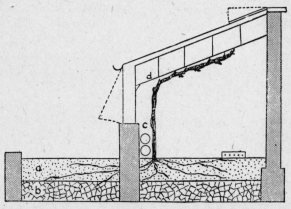

1. *Lean-to house for vines or peaches.* a, *border soil;* b, *drainage;* c, *hot-water pipes;* d, *training wires.*

a great age, and to keep them growing in a healthy condition over a number of years it is absolutely essential to start them off in the right soil.

The Loam. If the border has to be made up, the best kind of soil is a medium turfy loam with plenty of fibre in it, cut from an old pasture or downland, and stacked grass side downwards for a few months to rot down. When it is stacked, some well-rotted cow or horse manure should be added, in the proportion of about one part of manure to seven of loam, and a 5-in. potful of lime to each barrowload should also be added, except where the loam is cut from chalk or limestone land, when the addition of lime will be unnecessary.

Inside or Outside Border? The border may be made either inside or outside the house, or partly in and partly out. If it is the aim to ripen grapes early in the season, then the border should be inside, so that the border soil will warm up early in the season when the vines are started. For mid-season and late grapes an outside border can be quite satisfactory. Often it might be more suitable to the amateur to have the border outside, for example, where it is wished to grow grapes in a conservatory attached to the living-house.

When there is to be an outside border, it is of course necessary to make holes through the front wall, about the width of a brick, to bring the rod through into the house, and when the border is partly inside and partly outside, holes about 18 in. wide and down to the drainage must be made in the front wall below ground level, to allow the roots to grow freely outwards, which they seem inclined

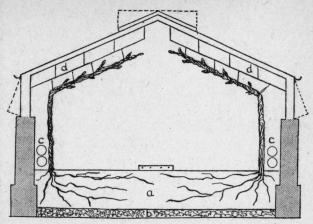

2. *Span house for vines or peaches.* a, *border soil;*
b, *drainage;* c, *hot-water pipes;* d, *training wires.*

to do when given the chance. This tendency on the part
of the roots to find a way outside, by forcing their way
either through or under the vinery wall and into cold wet
subsoil outside, sometimes leads to trouble which may be
in the form of shanking or split berries, or the failure of
the berries to colour properly. If this does happen, the
remedy lies in digging down on the outside of the house,
cutting through any roots found, and sealing with cement
any apertures found in the wall. This, of course, applies
only to an inside border.

Drainage. Efficient drainage is essential, and if the natural
drainage is not good enough, then resort must be made to
artificial means by placing at the bottom of the planting
hole or, if a border is to be made, under the whole area of

13

this, a 6-in. layer of broken bricks, with a drain or drains to lead surplus water away to a suitably lower spot in the garden.

If this method is not practicable owing to the lie of the land, then a soak-away might be constructed. To make this take out a good-sized hole about 5 ft. in depth and about the same distance across, and fill it with coarse rubble, broken brick, clinkers, etc., leading the drain from the border into it. Another method is to make the border up to a somewhat higher level than the surrounding land. If the site of the proposed planting lies very low, the raising of the border will most probably be essential.

Soil and Construction of Borders. Some garden soils are good enough for the successful cultivation of vines. The worst type is a heavy clay, which will always lie wet and cold, and in which the vines' roots will not ramify with ease, and in fact any roots which might be made at the start would probably die in a short while. On the other hand, a light sandy soil is not too good, as it dries out rapidly in the summer, and is usually deficient in plant nutrients.

The best type of soil is a good, deep, medium loam overlying gravel or sand, or limestone. This might be improved by digging it deeply, adding and mixing well as the work proceeds, $\frac{1}{4}$-in. bones or coarse bonemeal, at the rate of 2 lb. to the square yard, a good amount of lime rubble and some wood ash and charcoal. Cow or stable manure will be best applied as a mulch when the vines are growing freely.

In days gone by, it was always the thing to make a

border with turfy loam rotted down as mentioned on page 12. Some head gardeners of old, I understand, used to wait for a horse to die on the estate, and this was buried under the border.

This border should be made, approximately, the same width as the width of the house, be the border inside or outside, and if part of it is inside and part outside, the width inside plus the width outside should equal the width of the house.

The drainage material should be covered with newly cut turves, placed grass side downwards, to prevent the finer soil from working down into the drainage.

The stacked loam should be cut down with a spade, and the following ingredients added. To each barrow-load of loam add a 6-in. potful of each of coarse bonemeal and a proprietary vine manure, and a shovelful each of mortar rubble and wood ash or bonfire ash. Coarse sand may be used in the place of the mortar rubble if the latter is not available. No further farmyard manure should be added now, that which was added at the time of stacking the loam will be sufficient. The border should be made to a depth of from $2\frac{1}{2}$ to 3 ft., and of course the existing soil will have to be removed to this depth. As the new soil is put in, it should be made firm by treading.

Slope the Border. If the border is to be an outside one, then the old soil need not be excavated so deeply, as the border should be a raised one, and also sloping from the house outwards and downwards. There are very good reasons for making the border with a sloping surface, running towards the sun. It will ensure that the border will obtain the fullest benefit from any sun that shines in the early spring, and the warming up of the soil at this early date will help the roots of the vines to start away into vigorous growth. To warm the soil it used to be the practice in private gardens to cover the outside borders with a really good coating of fresh stable manure, up to as much as 18 in. in depth. This generated quite a fair amount of heat, over a period of time, and was also beneficial in keeping out of the border excessive amounts of cold rain, after the roots had become active. About the middle of May the bulk of this dressing would be removed to allow the increasing heat of the sun to have its beneficial effect upon the border. The slope on the border also permits excessive rain to be drained away, sometimes with the aid of sheets of galvanized iron, at the time when the grapes are hanging ripe on the vines.

This care of the border is very important. The soil is the medium through which the vines obtain their sustenance. All feeding of the plants has to be done through the soil, and the plant foods can only be taken up by the plant's roots in liquid form. Therefore it will be seen how very important is the mechanical condition of the soil. It should be fairly retentive of moisture, but at the same time so well drained that excessive water is taken quickly away, so that at no time is there danger of waterlogging, which would quickly cause the death of many roots.

PLANTING

When to Plant. The planting of dormant vines under glass may be carried out at any time during the autumn, or early in the spring, say up till the end of February. It is not wise to plant in mid-winter; far better to do it at a time when the formation of new roots will take place quickly. If the young vines for planting are not being grown at home, then suitable planting rods should be obtained from a reputable nurseryman. They are usually pot-grown, and sent out ex-pots with the soil still attached to the roots.

When planting in an inside border, instead of doing the job in the winter, it may if desired be carried out during May or early June, when the vines are actively growing. In this case it is better to have the young plants growing in boxes, about 4 or 5 in. deep, when the planting can be done without disturbance of the roots, which would be undesirable when actively growing.

Planting. When growing in the pots the roots will have grown in a circular fashion, therefore before planting the soil should be removed by washing it out in tepid water, disentangling the roots as much as possible, so that they may be straightened out and spread when planting. Place the roots carefully more or less horizontally in layers at differing depths, taking care that some of the finer soil is in direct contact with them everywhere, and tread firmly as the hole is filled in.

Planting should be at about the depth shown by the old soil mark.

Planting Distances. The distance at which to plant, if more than one vine is to be planted, will depend on what method of training is to be adopted. If single rods are to be taken, about 3 ft. apart or rather more is a reasonable distance, but if double rods are to be grown, a distance of 5 ft. should be allowed between vines.

In days gone by when much more care and detailed attention could be bestowed upon their cultivation than can today, some growers allowed as much as 5 ft. between when planting, even when only a single rod was to be taken up from each vine.

Watering. When planting is completed, give enough tepid water in the vicinity of the roots to settle them in, preferably applying it from a can with a coarse rose. Do not water all the border at this time, it would be of no use to the vines, and would merely tend to sour the soil.

Cutting Back and Disbudding. After planting, the rods should be cut well back, but this should not be done later than the middle of January, or bleeding may result, with subsequent loss of sap, and a considerable weakening of the new growth. After the middle of January, surplus buds above the point from which it is intended to take up new growth should be rubbed out as they start to develop, cutting away the surplus cane above the new shoot, when the latter has developed enough to take up all the sap. By cutting well back, even to within about four buds of the base, the new growth from this point will grow away strongly, as the roots become established in the new border.

Mulching. After planting is completed, a mulch of stable manure, or good compost, will be of benefit, and this applies especially to an outside border, or to summer planting inside.

18

CHAPTER THREE

ROUTINE CULTIVATION

ROD TRAINING AND MANAGEMENT

THE treatment of young vines after planting and of established older vines will always demand a good deal of care and attention to arrive at any degree of success. Most varieties of vines are free bearing, and the aim of the grower must be to induce the vines to produce the best they are capable of in quantity and quality. The habit of fruiting in vines is that the bunches are borne on the young shoots of the current season, which grow from buds produced during the previous season on the lateral growths, or on the main rod. The rods may be trained to what is known as the short-spur system, the long rod, or the extension—they will fruit equally well on any of these.

The Short-spur System. The short-spur system is the one most commonly adopted, and is the easiest and most straightforward in practice. With established vines, prune the laterals back to one or at the most two buds each season (Fig. 3). When building up the rods from freshly planted young vines, allow about 2 ft. of new rod each season till the required length is attained. The leading growth is allowed to grow to the top of the vinery each season and pruned back in the winter.

The buds which form in the axils of the leaves on these young rods will develop into lateral growths the next season; many of them, if not all, will produce embryo fruit bunches, and in the course of years these lateral growths will extend farther and farther from the rod, and will form what is known as the spurs, hence the name from which the spur system is derived. On very old vines these spurs will extend as much as 18 in. from the rod. It is not possible to shorten these spurs by pruning them

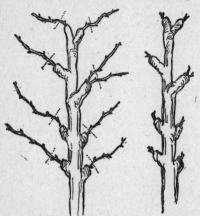

3. *Pruning.* Left: *section of vine showing laterals.* Right: *the same section after pruning.*

back into old cane, as they will not produce growths except from the young wood made during the previous season. If it is felt desirable to replace very old rods with young growth, the remedy lies in taking up a suitable young growth from the bottom, and when it is sufficiently developed the old rod may be cut completely away.

The Long-rod System. The long-rod system is carried out as follows. After planting, the young rod is cut back hard to near the base, and two growths are selected and trained upwards during the growing season. At pruning time the strongest rod is left to produce laterals and fruit the following season, the weakest one is again cut right back, to two or three buds, and again two rods are trained up, and the procedure of leaving the strongest and cutting back the weakest is carried out year after year. The rod which has carried the fruit is also cut out completely.

This system is practised chiefly by some exhibitors of the grape. Larger bunches can often be produced on these young vigorous rods, but it can be assumed that a larger total weight of fruit can be gathered from the spur system, from the same amount of space.

The Extension System. The extension system consists of letting one vine cover a large area by developing several main rods from the one root, and from these spurs are allowed to develop as in the spur system. The vine is planted at the end of the house, and the training may take the form of either taking several rods along the length of the house, or of taking one main rod along the bottom of the house, at the height of the eaves, and then taking subsidiary rods upwards at suitable distances throughout the house. One of the most famous vines in the country, which covers a very large area, is the one at Hampton Court, which is of the variety Black Hamburgh. This vine is very old, but it still produces annually a heavy weight of good-quality grapes.

STARTING THE VINES

This term is one used among growers to describe the starting of the vines into active growth in the spring by closing the ventilators of the house and raising the temperature either by artificial heating or natural sun heat. An increase of humidity in the atmosphere by damping down the floor and syringeing the vines with tepid water will induce the dormant buds to swell and break more readily. Up to the time of closing the house, the vines should have been afforded a thorough rest. A period of about three months is desirable, and this resting is brought about by keeping the borders fairly dry but not too dry, and by leaving the ventilators open as much as possible day and night, even allowing some frost on them, taking care that no harm comes to the heating system on this account.

When to Start. The time of starting will vary, and will be governed by several factors: if the varieties are early or late, if ripe grapes are required early or later, and if artificial heat is available or not. When it is decided to close the house, the border, if an inside one, should be examined for moisture content, and watered accordingly with tepid water. Let this watering be thorough, a good guide being that the border will not have received too much as long as water does not lie on the surface. The border will not require a further watering for some time, except perhaps in the immediate vicinity of the hot-water pipes. Where ripe grapes are required very early in the season, say by May or June, the house will be started as early as December, but not many private gardens and amateur growers will attempt anything so early as this under present-day conditions. About the end of January or early February is a good time to start for the earliest supply, and for this some artificial heat will be necessary, not a great deal perhaps, but enough to keep the vines moving along steadily once growth has started.

Temperatures. A suitable temperature when starting a vinery in February is about 45° F., and after a few weeks this should be raised by 5° to 10°. With sun heat it will doubtless rise more, and if it goes over 70°, a little air should be admitted through the top ventilator. When starting a vinery in March, the temperature can be about 50° to 55° F. at the beginning, as there will be more natural heat then and more light, and after three or four weeks it can be raised to 60° to 65° F.

Ventilation. Make it a rule always to admit some air as the temperature rises towards 70° F. Once the house has been closed, very little air will be needed for the first few weeks, it being well to remember the old saying, 'As the days lengthen, the cold strengthens', and we know only too well how so often this is true during January and February. On very sunny mornings a little top air may be needed, but the house should be closed early, soon after midday, to trap as much sun heat as possible.

As the season advances, the time of closing will have to be put back a little, but the actual time of closing down will have to be governed by the conditions prevailing on each particular day. In the early part of this century and before, when large private gardens were enjoying their more spacious days, many of the head gardeners of that time who were great plantsmen and grew many things well, in spite of having no great scientific knowledge, which at the present time is considered by many to be the beginning and end of growing, looked upon the production of first-class grapes as a real test of their ability. The admission of air and closing down of the vineries was a religion with them, and day in and day out, Saturdays and Sundays included, the man in charge had to carry out these operations at the precise moment, increasing and decreasing the amount of ventilation throughout the day as the outside temperature fluctuated. I have heard of a journeyman being instructed by the head gardener to sit in a vinery, waiting to operate the ventilators immediately a cloud passed over the sun. This meticulousness was in operation chiefly in early spring through February, March and April, when the sun can have considerable power, and at the same time the air can be very cold. Of course these things have to be managed in a much more general way nowadays. Perhaps for the amateur grower, who is away from home for the day, the answer to his greenhouse ventilation problems will be to fit one of the new extractor fans, and if a thermostatic control is also fitted, then ventilation becomes completely automatic. I have read of people using this system with complete satisfaction.

Maintaining Humidity. To ensure the buds of vines breaking freely, it is essential that there is plenty of humidity in the atmosphere of the house, therefore the paths and surface of the border should be damped down at least once a day, in the early morning, as well as at midday if outside conditions are not too cold. The vines should also be syringed with tepid water in the morning, but on no account must they be syringed with cold water.

As the season advances and warmth increases, the syringeing may be done in the afternoon as well, and damping down may be done more frequently.

Tying Down the Rods. So that there will be an even distribution of sap throughout, and the buds will break evenly, it is sometimes advised that young rods be tied downwards at the start, so that the whole length is about the same level. As soon as ever the buds start to grow, the rods must be taken up and tied in their final position.

Disbudding. As soon as it can be clearly seen which buds are growing freely, disbudding must be attended to. This consists in the removal of surplus growths. As a general rule one lateral growth to each spur is sufficient, the spurs being situated at intervals of from 9 in. to 12 in. up each side of the rod.

In some instances it is advisable to leave the removal of the surplus growths until the embryo fruit bunches show. This applies where it is desired to retain the largest bunches and where the variety in question is a shy bearer, and does not produce fruit on nearly every lateral as the free-bearing varieties do. As the fruit bunches show themselves, the laterals should be stopped by pinching out the point of the growth at two leaves beyond the bunch (Fig. 4), and any subsequent growths (sub-laterals) which push out should be stopped at one leaf.

FLOWERING TIME

As the vines come into flower, the atmosphere in the vinery should be kept somewhat drier to permit the pollen to be drier and in a more easily distributed condition, and

4. *A vine at flowering time.*

therefore the damping down in the morning should be
omitted, but if the weather is hot, some damping down of
the paths could be done after midday, when pollination
for the day has been carried out. Syringeing of the vines
is also normally suspended at this period, but with shy
setters some growers do syringe the bunches, and this
should be carried out by applying a fine spray with some
force directly on to the bunches in the early morning.

Pollination. Some varieties of grapes are free setters, and
some are shy setters. In the free setters, the pollen-bearing
anthers are carried erect on the flowers, and a tap on the
rods will displace the pollen and cause it to fall on the
pistil, which is situated in the middle of and below the
level of the anthers, thereby carrying out the pollination.

26

In the shy setters the anthers, instead of being erect, are pendulous, thereby falling below the level of the pistil, and the pollen-bearing organs in these shy setters are often enclosed with a cap, which is not easily dislodged. The syringeing mentioned earlier helps to dislodge these caps, thereby freeing the pollen. The reason for syringeing early in the morning is to give time for the pollen to dry by midday.

There are several methods by which the pollination of grapes under glass may be carried out, but the one usually adopted is to give the rods a sharp tap, using the hand for the bottom of the rods and a firm rod for the tops. This is all that is needed for free-setting varieties. For the shy setters, of which that excellent variety, Muscat of Alexandria, is an example, something a little different often needs to be carried out to get a good set. Running over the flowers with a rabbit or hare's tail is practised by some, and some growers I know use the palm of their hand, drawing it very gently over the bunch. A soft hand and a gentle touch is needed when employing this method. Again, some growers collect pollen from free-bearing varieties (shaking it on to a piece of glass is a good way) and then apply it to the variety to be pollinated. A hare's tail may be used to do this, or it may be gently blown from the glass surface over the bunch. It helps a good deal if a free variety can be grown with shy ones, and you should try to get them to flower at approximately the same time, but pollen can be collected, and if it is kept in a tightly closed tin or box, it will remain potent for two or three weeks. The Muscat varieties in general are mostly shy setters, and the poorer-quality ones, such as Black Hamburgh, Alicante, Gros Colmar, are the free setters.

How pleasant it is to enter a vinery when grapes are in flower. They have one of the most lovely scents imaginable.

Training. It is usual for a vinery to be furnished with wires running from end to end, passed through eyes fixed in the roof rafters, on which the vines are trained. These wires should be about 18 in. from the roof glass, and about 1 ft. apart. As the lateral growths become long enough, they should be secured to the wires by means of raffia ties. This operation needs to be done with care, getting them into their final position along the wires by easy stages. Some varieties tend to grow turgidly upwards, and if an attempt is made to pull them down suddenly, they will often snap or heel out at the base; the variety Black Hamburgh is very prone to do this.

Thinning. Not very long after the flowering period, the thinning of the bunches will have to be attended to. This operation consists in cutting out with special grape-thinning scissors all seedless berries, and other superfluous berries, mostly from the centre of the bunch (Fig. 5). The aim will be to ensure that when the bunch is finally thinned, when the berries have attained their full size, they will nicely fill all the space, without overcrowding. Seedless berries are easily distinguishable by the fact that they are much smaller than those with seeds, and will never attain much size.

This, I imagine, is where Nature takes a hand, as she is not inclined to waste resources where there are no seeds

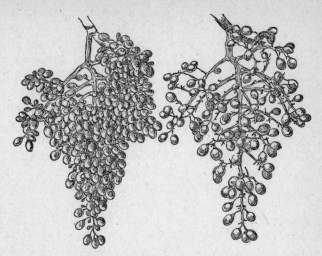

5. *Thinning.* Left: *a bunch of grapes unthinned.* Right: *the same bunch after thinning.*

to mature. When growing in the wild state, vines, in common with most plants, will rely on the production of seed for the perpetuation of the species, the problem with which Nature is always mostly concerned. It is usual for more bunches to be left to flower and set than will finally be left to develop. Therefore an assessment should be made of what the final number of bunches left should amount to, and any surplus ones removed before thinning is started. On the average a vine should carry 1 lb. to $1\frac{1}{2}$ lb. to each 1 ft. run of rod.

Thinning is an operation which calls for much care on

the part of the operator, to avoid causing superficial damage to the tender skins of the young grapes. For instance they must never be handled, nor must any rough materials such as clothes or hair of the head come into contact with them. It is a good plan to wear something soft over the head, such as a handkerchief or silk scarf, when thinning. On large commercial undertakings where grapes are grown, the job of thinning is carried on all through the day, and in such very large airy houses this is no great hardship, but in a small greenhouse, where there are only a few bunches to deal with, I thoroughly recommend the early mornings or evenings as the time to tackle this job. In a small greenhouse the sun can be overpowering in the middle of the day.

Thinning of free-setting varieties may be started safely at an earlier stage than is advisable with the shy setters. In the bunches of the latter there are often quite a number of seedless berries, but given a little time, the berries with seeds will grow away, and be easily distinguishable. Start thinning at the bottom of the bunch and work upwards, and to steady the bunch while working on it use a thin piece of cane, or a piece of raffia. When the bunches have shoulders, these should be tied up with raffia to the wires or laterals, in a slightly elevated position, somewhat in the style that the 'wide boys' like their jackets.

A good pair of shoulders (Fig. 6) is an asset to a bunch of grapes, and greatly improves the appearance! There are really no hard-and-fast rules for grape thinning, getting the best results will only come by experience, and

6. *A bunch of ripe grapes. Note the wide 'shoulders.'*

different varieties need their own particular treatment owing to the varying size of the berries when ripe.

Routine Management. After thinning, the young grapes will grow away rapidly, and at this time the watering of the border must be attended to regularly, and any feeding carried out which may be considered necessary. As the season advances into May and beyond, as the outside air becomes warmer, more air will need to be admitted, and damping down of the paths and borders carried out three times a day on sunny days—in the morning, at midday and late afternoon. The closing of the house will need to be left till late afternoon on sunny days, closing up earlier on dull days.

To ensure against scorching of the foliage and scalding of the berries, always put a little air on the top of the house, first thing in the morning, even on the dullest days from about the middle of April onwards. These troubles are brought about often when there is a sudden burst of hot sunshine and moisture still on the plants, which conditions obtain if the house is kept closed.

Shading. As the sun gains power and becomes higher in the heavens, it is usually advisable to supply a little shading in the form of light 'Summer Cloud', or in some instances heavy netting fixed on the roof glass will be sufficient. A lean-to house facing south will need more shading than will a span house running north and south. These observations chiefly apply to the south of England and the Midlands. In the north of England and Scotland shading will probably not be necessary, but wherever the grower might be living, whether shading is needed or not will depend largely on factors such as aspect, the pitch of the roof of the vinery, and how the vinery is orientated.

Black grapes when they are ripening, and while hanging ripe on the vines, require more shading than do white grapes, and it is often considered necessary to tie some of the foliage away from the bunches of white varieties, especially Muscat of Alexandria, to attain a more golden colouring in the berries. Some slight diffusion of the sun's rays will be necessary, a sheet of good-quality white tissue-paper fixed over the top of the bunches being good for the purpose. Some of the best coloured and best finished Muscat of Alexandria grapes I have seen were from Glamis Castle, the Scottish home of the Earl of Strathmore. They were grown by Mr MacInnes, the head gardener, who was a noted exhibitor of grapes over a great many years, and I believe I am right in stating they were grown without shading.

The Stoning Period. The stoning period is a slightly critical stage in the development of the berries, and occurs when they are about half grown. They appear to be at a standstill for some time, and the vines should be kept growing along steadily, and not excited into quick growth by feeding or high temperature. The stoning period safely past, the berries will swell away rapidly again, and a feed with a balanced vine manure should be given and well watered in. Watering must be done carefully and regularly, giving enough to meet the requirements of the vines, and being careful not to get the border over-wet or split berries may well result.

Ripening. The variety Madresfield Court is very susceptible to splitting of the skins at the ripening period, and calls for special care. Some air should be admitted through the ventilators top and front, all the time, and a little warmth should circulate through the hot-water pipes to maintain a warm, dry, buoyant atmosphere. No damping down must be done at this time, and it is advisable to cover the border with a good thick layer of dry straw to prevent damp rising from this. I have seen this variety recommended as being suitable for a cold greenhouse, but from experience I would say it is entirely unsuitable.

It is my opinion that if sufficient heat can be maintained in the hot-water pipes, then the problem of split berries is not likely to arise very much, but with the price of fuel at its present shocking high level, fires often have to be dispensed with on the grounds of economy. Covering all the borders with a thick layer of straw will help a great deal towards the prevention of split berries in other varieties, some of which are susceptible to this trouble. If the border is an outside one, it might well be necessary to cover it with sheets of galvanized iron or with wooden shutters, to ward off excessive amounts of rain.

Early varieties of grapes will hang for some time on the vines after ripening if it is desired to keep them back for a while, while late varieties, such as Alicante, Gros Colmar, Lady Downes, Mrs Pinces' Black Muscat and Muscat of Alexandria, will hang very much longer if properly managed, up to Christmas, or even in some conditions well into the New Year. When grapes are hanging ripe on the rods, the vinery should have air admitted at all times to maintain a buoyant atmosphere, and for later in the season some artificial heating will need to be on hand, to be brought into operation when conditions of damp or cold demand.

Keeping Ripe Grapes. Ripe grapes may be kept satisfactorily for a time when cut and placed in bottles of water in a suitably dry room. In large private gardens at one time it was customary to have a special heated grape room, usually an addition to the ordinary fruit room, for the purpose of keeping grapes when cut late in the season. Special racks were fitted, and special bottles made with a fairly wide upturned neck were used. Pieces of charcoal were placed in the water to prevent it from becoming putrid. If the amateur wishes to keep grapes in this way, he could probably fix up the necessary equipment in the kitchen, as a little warmth is usually required to keep the berries from rotting. Ordinary bottles could be used.

Keeping out Wasps. Wasps are great enemies of ripe grapes, and as grapes ripen, it becomes necessary in most seasons to exclude wasps from the vinery, by fixing securely over the ventilator apertures some suitable material, something light enough to allow plenty of air through. Tiffany or butter muslin is suitable for this purpose. Doors must be kept closed, or frames with wasp-excluding material fitted, made to fix into the doorways. In the 1955 season it was not necessary to carry out these precautions, as there was scarcely a wasp to be seen, and that despite the summer being so warm and dry.

Pruning. During the time the vines are dormant and completely at rest, pruning should be carried out, and I always like to do this around the shortest day. If pruning is done when there is any movement of sap, what is termed bleeding will take place, and a fair amount of sap will be lost, to the detriment of the new growths. To prevent bleeding, the wounds made when pruning should be treated with vine styptic, or with carpenter's knotting. With vines trained on the spur system, pruning consists in cutting back to one or two eyes the lateral growths made during the previous growing season (Fig. 4). The cutting out to be done in the long-rod system has been dealt with on page 20.

Cleaning. While the vines are at rest, some cleaning of the vines and the vinery should be carried out. The wood-work, iron-work and glass should be sprayed with hot soapy water with a little paraffin added, scrubbed well, and then washed down with clean water, using the hose or a syringe. If mealy bug has been present on the vines during the growing season, a careful examination should be made, scraping away with a knife any loose bark under which bugs may be lurking. The rods should then be washed with a nicotine mixture, or washed or sprayed with a 5 per cent. solution of tar-oil winter wash.

The time-honoured custom of painting the vines annually with a witch's brew, consisting of Gishurst compound, neat cow dung, sulphur, soot, a dash of nicotine, some clay or loam to make it stick well, is not much practised I think at the present time. This brew was mixed with water to the consistency of thick cream and applied with a brush to all parts of the rods, leaving only the eyes clear. It was, I am quite sure, effective in suppressing many insect enemies, and some held the view that it was of manurial benefit to the vines.

CHAPTER FOUR

RENOVATION AND RENEWAL OF BORDERS

RENOVATION

HOWEVER well borders may be made in the first instance, with the routine cultivations of surface manurings, and constant damping down in the growing season, they tend in time to become sour and inert, therefore an annual renovation of the surface soil is desirable to maintain the vines in a healthy condition. Some time during the winter the top soil of the border, to the depth of about 2 in., should be loosened by pricking carefully with a fork, taking care not to damage any roots which might be near the surface. This top soil should then be raked off with an iron rake and removed. Bonemeal at the rate of 4 oz. to the square yard, dried blood or hoof and horn meal at the same rate, and sulphate of potash at 2 oz. per square yard should be spread on the border and lightly forked in. Alternatively, a good specific vine manure such as Thompson's or Bentley's may be applied at the rate recommended by the makers. A dressing of new loam, cut from a pasture and stacked for a few months to rot down, should then be applied, and a light mulching of stable manure or well-rotted cow dung may also be added. This treatment of the border should be carried out annually.

RENEWAL

There may come a time when, after a good many years the border becomes exhausted, and the more drastic treatment of renewing the whole border is called for. If this is to be carried out, it should be done in the autumn, as the foliage begins to turn, while there is still time for the vines to make a little new root in the new soil before finally coming to complete rest for the winter.

Start on the side of the border farthest away from where the vines are planted, and with a digging fork work right down to the drainage, carefully preserving any live roots which may be encountered, wrapping them, temporarily, in damp sacking. Any dead roots should be cut away, going back to where they show life. If all the old soil can be taken away, and the border remade with a mixture of new soil made up as advised for planting young vines, that will be ideal, but if this amount of new loam is not available, then the vigour of the vines would be restored, to a certain extent, by partial renovation, that is, adding some new loam in with some of the old border soil, and adding a liberal dressing of coarse bone-meal, a good vine manure, and some well broken up old mortar rubble if obtainable. Examine the drainage while the soil is clear of it, and if necessary clean it out and replace it, covering it with turves from pasture, as advised for making a new border. When making the border up again, as the level rises carefully replace the vine roots horizontally, bearing in mind that those nearest the surface are the ones which will become active again most readily.

When the job of replanting is completed, give the border a good watering, to settle the soil well round the roots, give a mulching of fresh strawy stable manure if available, or failing this, partially composted straw. Keep the vines well syringed to help them to re-establish. I should have mentioned that, of course, all fruit should be cut before starting this operation.

CHAPTER FIVE

CULTURE IN POTS AND TUBS

THE growing of vines in large pots in orchard houses is quite usual, but I will deal with it more from the point of view of the amateur, who might not be able to manage a vine border, but could find room for a vine in a pot or tub. If it is desired that no time be lost, then a fruiting-size vine established in a pot may be purchased from a specialist nurseryman, and grapes may be cut the season following purchase, or a younger cane may be bought, at a less cost, and grown on for a season, before letting it fruit. Or a start may be made by growing on one's own from an eye (see Chapter Seven). It is possible by this method to have a couple of bunches of grapes in the second year, if the cane is grown on strongly enough the first year, or it can be grown for two years before taking fruit.

Potting. The soil for these pots should be the same as recommended for the borders, with a more generous admixture of bonemeal and other manures. If the smaller-size cane is purchased, it will be delivered some time during the winter or early spring, and if it comes ex-pot, it should be repotted straightway, either in one of similar size to the one it came out of (probably 7 in. or 8 in.) and then potted on into a larger one in early summer when it has made some growth, or it could be potted into a 10-in. size straightway and left to grow the whole season in this. If it is decided to start from eyes, they should be started off in a 4-in. or 5-in. pot, or possibly started in a seed tray and potted up when roots have formed. When they are growing away well in this size pot, pot them on into a 6-in. or 7-in. for the first season. The following season when they have made some growth, pot them on into a 10-in. The next season they could be left to fruit in this size, carrying two or three bunches, and for the season following that, potted on into a 12-in. or a tub of similar size, when they could be allowed to carry six or eight bunches, and should then do this annually.

Routine Management. An annual top dressing of good soil should be given, working off the top few inches of old soil with a pointed stick, and replacing it with new soil. Growing in this restricted amount of soil, the plants must be well fed and well watered during the growing season.

They may be given fairly frequent applications of weak liquid manure, an occasional dusting of dried blood well watered in, and what is of special benefit to pot-grown fruits, a top dressing during the growing season, of a mixture of horse droppings and spent hops. To hold this in position on top of the pots, zinc bands 3 or 4 in. wide may be used. These pot vines should be grown in a greenhouse exactly as those planted in borders. When the fruit has been cut, they can be stood outside for a time, but it is not advisable to leave them out during very hard frost, and they should therefore be put back in a cold greenhouse around Christmas. Good strong bamboo canes 5 ft. high should be used to support the vines and to make a framework on which to tie the lateral growths.

CHAPTER SIX

PESTS, DISEASES AND PHYSIOLOGICAL DISORDERS

MOST of the troubles which arise with grapes growing under glass are usually due to incorrect management and culture.

PESTS

Mealy Bug. Often mealy bug is introduced on some other plant. This pest does not seem to be so prevalent as it was formerly. A stove house and certain of its plant inhabitants was always a happy breeding-ground for it, but now stove houses are the exception.

If any bugs are detected during the growing season, they should be dabbed with a small stiff brush dipped in methylated spirit, or a strong solution of nicotine. Cotton-wool should be tied on the laterals each side of the bunches to prevent them moving in, and this will often prove a successful barrier. Tar-oil winter wash applied during the dormant season will often prove a good control.

Red Spider. If red spider should make an appearance, it is usually due to too dry conditions. Plenty of moisture in the atmosphere, introduced by damping two or three times daily, and syringeing twice daily till the vines flower, missing this routine only when outside conditions are wet and cold. Sulphur is a good deterrent to red spider, and the house should be given a good do with the sulphur vaporizer when the vines are dormant.

Thrips. Thrips, another leaf enemy, can be troublesome, and fumigating with nicotine is the remedy.

Rats, Mice and Birds. Rats and mice can do a lot of damage to ripe grapes, and it might be some time before the trouble is suspected, as they climb the rods with ease, feeding on top of the bunches.

They must be exterminated by traps and poison, using 'Warfarin' for the poison, as this is safer to use. A robber robin will sometimes cause trouble by developing a liking for ripe grapes, and he should be excluded from entering the vinery in the same way as with the wasps.

DISEASES

Mildew. This is one of the most usual diseases of vines, often caused by too much moisture allied with too low a temperature, or by admitting cold air through the ventilators early in the season. Flowers of sulphur dusted round the house and over the rods and young growths will usually cure the trouble, or the sulphur vaporizer may be brought into action, which will be the more effective means of control.

PHYSIOLOGICAL DISORDERS

Shanking. This is a physiological disorder in which the green fruit stalks shrivel and turn brown before the berries ripen. The trouble is attributed to several different causes, such as overcropping, too drastic defoliation, and the roots getting down into cold subsoil. The latter is the

43

most probable cause, and I have already mentioned the remedy on page 13.

Scorching. Scorching of the foliage is caused by too high temperature from sun heat inside the vinery, and usually occurs when the foliage is wet. It can happen in the morning by allowing the temperature to rise too high before admitting air, or in the afternoon by closing the house too early. A skilled grape grower can smell scorch in a house as soon as he enters if it has occurred.

Scalding. Scalding of the berries is caused by the same factors as scorching, but usually occurs in the morning, when it will be noticed there is a film of moisture on them, caused through the berries becoming cold overnight, and if hot sun catches them in this condition, the rapid change from cold to heat causes a rupture of the skin tissues. The most usual time for this trouble to occur is during stoning, and the remedy lies in admitting a little air first thing in the morning to dispel the moisture from the surface of the berries.

CHAPTER SEVEN

PROPAGATION

Vines may be propagated by either seeds, eyes, grafts, or layering. They are only raised from seed when it is desired to raise a new variety, and this method is not of general interest to the amateur.

Propagation from Eyes. The simplest and most practical method is to raise young canes from eyes (Fig. 5). These are saved when pruning, and the laterals can be plunged out of doors in peat till required. Choose good plump buds, and cut them with about $\frac{1}{2}$ in. of wood on either side. Insert them singly in a 3-in. pot with the eye uppermost just below the soil level. Let the soil be a light mixture of loam leaf-mould and sand. They can go in any time during January or early in February. If possible place them in a propagating case with bottom heat, but they will grow, although more slowly, if placed in the open greenhouse (Fig. 7). If they can be grown in strong heat all through, they would make a cane 6 ft. or 8 ft. long at the end of the first summer, but in the heat available to most people, a cane about 3 ft. can be looked for. When the eyes have made sufficient growth and roots, pot them on in a good mixture into 6-in. or 7-in. pots. The following season pot them on into a larger pot, and if it is intended for them to be planted in a border, this may be done during the summer, when they are in full growth, or kept in the pot till the autumn and planted then.

7. *Propagation.*
An eye cutting
rooted and
growing.

About midsummer the growing point of the young cane should be pinched out, when it is about 6 or 7 ft. high, so that it may become well ripened. At the end of the first year's growth the young rod should be cut down to near ground level, and this must be repeated at the end of the second year, if rod production is the chief aim. If grapes are desired, then it must be left 5 or 6 ft. in length, at the end of the second year.

Grafting. The grafting of vines is fairly easy and successful, and may be used for the purpose of introducing a different variety on to an existing rod, or for putting what is considered to be rather a weak-growing variety on to the root stock of one of the stronger-growing ones, viz: Black Hamburgh, Alicante, or Muscat of Alexandria. The latter, in spite of being the best flavoured grape, is also a vigorous grower, and it is considered that it imparts

46

some of its own good flavour to varieties grafted on to it. Whip and tongue grafting is the best method to employ for grapes. The scion should be a good strong one-year-old growth, and if the graft is to be put on a young cane, the two should be as near as possible alike in size.

The scions for the grafting must be taken during the dormant season and heeled in out of doors. Any cutting back of the stock must be done in the normal pruning season, and about two buds should be left above where the graft is going on. These should be allowed to grow

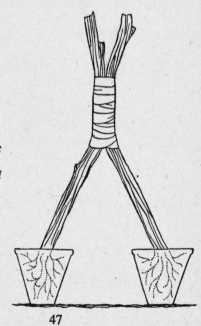

8. *Grafting by approach. The vine on the left provides the stock, that on the right the scion. The bud on the top right will grow into a new vine, and the scion is cut off just below the raffia tie when it is growing freely.*

for a short while after the graft is put on, stopping them at two leaves. The time to do the grafting is when growth is just starting in the stock, and the scion should be brought into a warm temperature for about a week before the operation. When the scion is growing freely, that part of the stock above the union may be competely removed.

Inarching or Grafting by Approach. This is a very good method to adopt for vines, and both the stock and scion may be growing in pots (Fig. 8) or the scion only, and in either case it is the easiest matter to get the stock and scion into juxta-position. If the grafting is to be done on an old vine, it will be best to work on to a strong lateral growth situated at the bottom end of the vine. The normal practices of grafting must be carried. The cambium layers must be together exactly, the stock and scion bound tightly together with raffia, and the whole union covered in completely with grafting wax, to exclude air.

CHAPTER EIGHT

VARIETIES FOR GREENHOUSE CULTURE

THE varieties of grapes are numerous, but I shall only include the fairly well-known varieties. It is doubtful if some of the good varieties grown forty years ago and more are procurable at the present day. There was often allotted for grapes in the early years of this century an early house, a mid-season house, a Muscat house and a late house, and a very comprehensive collection of varieties was grown.

Alicante. A strong-growing late black variety. The bunches are large, with large shoulders. The berries are large, oval in shape, with a tough skin, but the flavour is not good. It will grow quite well in a cool house, but is better flavoured where grown with a little heat. It is moderately fruitful.

Black Hamburgh. This is the amateur's grape *par excellence*. It is a strong grower, fruitful, with large, sometimes very large bunches. If left hanging till very ripe, the flavour becomes rich and very good. It is most accommodating, as it can be forced early, will grow well in a cool house, is excellent for pot work, is good for exhibition, and will grow outdoors on a warm wall. It has been recorded that a bunch of this variety has been grown weighing $21\frac{1}{2}$ lb.

Muscat Hamburgh. A grape of the Hamburgh type with

Muscat flavour. It is a shy setter, so should be set with the pollen of Black Hamburgh. Can be grown in either the cool house or with Muscats.

Bowood Muscat. This variety is a Muscat of Alexandria type. It produces a large-shouldered bunch with large berries, of true Muscat flavour, rich and sweet. It has the virtue of being freer in setting than Muscat of Alexandria.

Buckland Sweetwater. This is a good white grape for the early and mid-season house, and should be given the same treatment as Black Hamburgh. It is a pleasing grape to eat, the berries are fairly large, with a thin skin, of a nice golden colour when fully ripe, and are juicy and sweet. Requires some assistance in setting.

Canon Hall Muscat. A difficult grape to grow, being a bad setter, and pollination must be effected with pollen from a free setter. It is a form of Muscat of Alexandria, having longer bunches and bigger berries than the type. When well fertilized the bunches are handsome in appearance, but being so capricious, it is one for the expert.

Foster's Seedling. One of the Sweetwater white grapes, suitable for early or mid-season, and very good for growing in pots. Requires the same treatment as Black Hamburgh. The bunches are fairly large, and the berries juicy and sweet. To get the best colour, the bunches should be exposed to the sun.

Gros Colmar. A strong-growing late grape of poor quality. It is grown very extensively for market, because of its appearance and ease of culture. The berries are very large, almost round, black, with thick skin. It is a free setter, and thinning should be done early and with a free hand. It is claimed that the flavour is improved if grafted on to Muscat of Alexandria, and given Muscat treatment.

Barbarossa. A late black grape, of indifferent quality, but mentioned because of the enormous size of the bunches (it is reported that a bunch of this variety was grown in Ireland weighing over 23 lb.). It will hang very late, and then it will be at its best for eating.

Lady Downes. This is one of the better-quality late black grapes. It is fruitful but prone to scalding at the stoning period, needing special care at that time. It has great keeping qualities, but in common with most late grapes, it needs Muscat treatment to get it well finished and reasonably early in the autumn, which is necessary to produce good quality.

Madresfield Court. A black grape, early or mid-season, but not suitable for late. It is one of the leading varieties, especially good for exhibition. The bunches are large, shapely and well proportioned, with large berries long oval in shape. The flesh is juicy and rich, with Muscat flavour. It is recommended as suitable for a cool vinery, but under these conditions trouble is likely to arise, owing to the susceptibility to split berries at the final swelling.

Muscat of Alexandria. Without doubt the best grape. It is a robust grower, very fruitful, the bunches are large, the best ones having good shoulders, the berries are large with firm flesh, the richest of all grapes, with a pronounced and to most people a delicious musk flavour. Reference has already been made as to its being a shy

51

setter, but given the necessary attention in the matter of fertilization, this can be overcome.

To do it well it must be afforded what is known as Muscat treatment, which means artificial heat at least for starting and up to the time after the fruits are set, and then again at the ripening period to get good finish. It may happen that at times in midsummer pipe heat can be dispensed with during the warmer spells. The variety has, I know, been grown fairly well without fire heat during some of the more favourable summers, and during the war years growers sometimes were forced to grow without. When they are being grown cool the vines should not be started earlier than the end of February.

Mrs Pince's Black Muscat. This is a very good quality late-keeping black grape, with large bunches, the berries being of medium size. It requires strong heat to finish well. It is a high pointing exhibitor's grape, and I have seen excellent bunches of this shown by the late Mr F. Rose of Townhill Park.

There are many other varieties one might mention, but present-day conditions do not permit of the growing of comprehensive collections, as was the custom years ago, more is the pity.

CHAPTER NINE

GRAPES OUT OF DOORS

BY R. BARRINGTON BROCK

THE Viticultural Research Station at Oxted, Surrey, has been carrying out experiments on the cultivation of grapes for eating and wine, out of doors, for ten years, and some most interesting and satisfactory results have been achieved.

The requirements for outdoor cultivation are completely different from the requirements in cold or hot houses. Immediately a vine is put in a cold or hot house, it is effectively operating in a warmer climate, and the fundamental requirement for all pruning out of doors is to reduce the size of the vine progressively as the climate gets colder and colder. For this reason it is possible to have very large vines fruiting satisfactorily in houses, but out of doors the vines are always kept very short and with a minimum of old wood.

This generalization applies to both eating and wine varieties and even to cloche cultivation. We have had particularly satisfactory results under cloches with high-grade eating grapes and the highest-quality wine grapes, but only by developing a method of pruning which is specifically suited for cloches. It might be possible to use a vine under a cloche, pruned on the style of a cold-house vine, but in general it has not seemed so satisfactory and is rather against the general findings of our work.

It is difficult to give very explicit instructions in pruning for the open ground and for cloches in a short chapter, but the research station holds Open Days each autumn, so that anybody particularly interested in learning the details and examining the various types of vine under growing conditions, can apply in the summer to come on the Open Days.

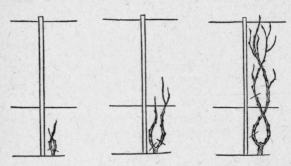

9. *Pruning.* Left: *1st year.* Centre: *2nd year.*
Right: *3rd year.*

Pruning. There are many methods of pruning possible for outdoor vines, but in the colder climates it is essential that the vine itself shall be kept small and the crop per vine also relatively small. It should be borne in mind that under good conditions an outdoor vine will bear two or three times the quantity of fruit which it can safely ripen, and it is necessary to be very drastic in removing all but a reasonable number of bunches, e.g. 6 to 12 on an established vine. If one is too greedy, many vines are even capable of fruiting themselves to death.

We normally adopt a method of pruning known as

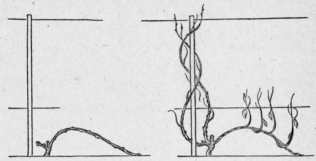

10. *Pruning.* Left: *3rd year* Guyot pruned. Right: *4th summer*—leave only 2 or 3 bunches.

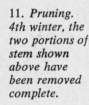

11. *Pruning. 4th winter, the two portions of stem shown above have been removed complete.*

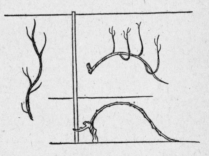

Guyot, because this is applicable to any type of vine and lends itself most particularly to cloche work. It is a very simple system, and in essence consists of using a fresh complete shoot every year and cutting off all the old wood. The illustrations show (Figs. 9, 10, 11) the principle of the method and it has proved very simple to operate. Do not be disturbed by the thought that by this means your stem is always lengthening and will soon get too long. In healthy vines there are always a large number of unwanted shoots from the base, and when the stem is getting too long, one of these shoots can be left in to form the fruiting shoot for the next year, and all the old stem can be safely cut away in the winter, so that the vine virtually starts afresh.

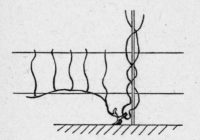

12. *Pruning. Modified Guyot method, in which the bearing shoot is trained on a bottom wire 8 to 10 in. from the ground.*

The original scheme, as shown in these illustrations, frequently caused the bunches of grapes which are borne above the third or fourth leaf on the shoots to come too near the ground, where they were splashed with mud in thunder-storms. We have lately adopted a slightly modified Guyot method whereby the bearing shoot is trained on a bottom wire about 8 to 10 in. from the ground. This brings the bunches about 18 in. from the ground, which is very satisfactory, and is shown in Fig. 12.

Culture under Tomato Cloches. It will be seen, of course, that this Guyot method brings shoots to a very good height for operation underneath tomato cloches, and we have evolved a method which works extremely well. In this method the fruiting shoots from the horizontal bearing canes are trained up and out of the side of the cloche, as shown in Fig. 13. They are then topped three or four leaves above the top of the cloche, and after this they throw out fresh shoots from every leaf joint. We have

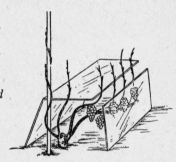

13. *Under tomato cloches. The fruiting shoots are trained up and out of the side of the cloche, then topped 3 or 4 leaves above the top of the cloche.*

found that it is completely successful if one merely rubs out all these new shoots *inside* the cloche, leaving only the original leaves and the bunches of fruit on the fruiting stems. The new shoots, however, on the parts of the stem *outside* the cloche are retained and pinched out or chopped off repeatedly, so that one gradually gets a great head of leaves outside the cloche, but the inside of the cloche remains relatively free of foliage and the bunches are hanging fairly clear. If this method is not adopted, one quickly gets an enormous thicket of leaves inside the cloche which effectively prevents air circulation and gives rise to mildew and rotting of the grapes.

Using this method, under tomato cloches, we have found that varieties ripen consistently between four and six weeks earlier than they do in the same localities in the open vineyard, and this means that it is possible to ripen a considerable number of the finest eating grapes with certainty, although these special varieties will normally only ripen in the open vineyard in two years out of five.

Grapes for Wine. All methods mentioned are practicable, whether the vines are for eating or wine, and in fact many of the varieties are suitable for both.

However, wine varieties usually have rather small berries and a very high proportion of juice, whereas the real eating varieties have been bred to have bigger berries which are meatier and therefore not so suitable for wine. All of them, of course, if they reach a sufficiently high sugar content, can be fermented to produce a wine, but in many cases the flavour will be disappointing, although the wine is usually drinkable. From the point of view of the wine maker, he is more interested in obtaining the greatest possible quantity of juice, and this is usually obtained by a large number of relatively small bunches of relatively small grapes rather than by a few bunches of very large grapes, which in any case are not usually very juicy.

Insect Pests. There are very few insects which appear to attack the vine in this country. The phylloxera, which devastated the vineyards of Europe many years ago, is not normally found in this country, and great efforts are being made to keep it out. It cannot, therefore, be over-emphasized how criminal it is to import any rooted vines whatsoever from abroad, as these almost always have the eggs in the roots. Cuttings which are received should always be sterilized, but are not so dangerous as the rooted vines which are almost always contaminated.

Fungus Diseases. The usual trouble with outdoor vines is fungus attack, which comes mainly in three forms. There is the powdery mildew (oidium), the downy mildew and the botrytis, which actually rots the grape berries. All these are worse in a wet year, and the universal method of treating them is to apply preventive sprays or powder at intervals. With cloche vines we normally use a 50:50 mixture of ground sulphur powder and Bordeaux powder. These can be puffed through any of the standard powder blowers. They only have to be puffed into the cloches here and there and the powder finds its way all over the vines and the fruit. The parts outside the cloche cannot be readily sprayed, but can be powdered very easily at the same time. In a wet season, however, this powder is washed off rather quickly, and it is necessary to apply the powder every week if it has all been washed off. It only takes a few moments, but where cloches are not being used, wet sprays are perfect because they do not have to be used so often.

In the open vineyard, the normal procedure is to powder with ground sulphur when the shoots are about 6 or 8 in. long and again when the flowers are in bloom. Immediately after blooming is over, a standard Bordeaux spray, as used for potatoes, is applied, and two further sprays at about four or six weeks' intervals are usually required.

It is not normally necessary to do any spraying after the end of August, and it will be found that the Bordeaux spray, if applied properly, has a wonderful power of adhesion, even after thunder-storms, etc. In many cold seasons it has not proved necessary to give any sulphur powder, and an early Bordeaux spray well before blossoming and then two more later ones have sometimes been sufficient, but in a warm wet season four sprays would normally be necessary.

VARIETIES FOR OUTDOOR CULTURE

Unfortunately, in the past a very high proportion of the English grown grapes have proved to be falsely named. This position is improved, but it is certainly advisable to take any opportunity of checking the actual names, when paying a visit to the Research Station. Alternatively, correctly named varieties can be purchased, from the Research Station, and used for comparison.

Of the hundreds of varieties which have been tested, the following are the recommendations at the moment, but these are constantly being modified as newer and better varieties are found:

For eating grapes in the open vineyard:
Precoce de Malingre.
Noir Hatif de Marseille.
Pirovano 14.
Muscat de Saumur.

Oliver Irsay.
Pearl of Czaba.

For eating grapes under cloches:
Precoce de Malingre.
Noir Hatif de Marseille.
Pirovano 14.
Muscat de Saumur.
Oliver Irsay.
Muscat Queen.
White Frontignan.
Chasselas 1921.
Chasselas Rose Royale.
Muscat Hamburgh.
Pearl of Czaba.

For wine grapes in the open vineyard:
Gamay Hatif des Vosges.
Pirovano 14.
Madeleine X. Sylvaner 28/51.
Riesling Sylvaner.
Seyve-Villard 5-276.
Precoce de Malingre.
Seibel 13053.

Part Two: Peaches and Nectarines

CHAPTER TEN

ORIGIN AND TYPES

Origin. It is now the generally accepted view that the types of peaches and nectarines now grown in gardens had their origin in China. Both are forms of *Prunus persica*, and the only difference between them is that the peach has a downy skin and the nectarine a smooth one. Although the trees of both under cultivation need identical treatment, it is generally found to be easier to produce good fruits of the peach than it is of the nectarine, especially when grown outdoors. China is the first country in which this fruit was cultivated thousands of years ago. This much has been gathered from old Chinese literature. The peach came westward from the Far East a very long time ago into Persia, Greece and Roman Italy. There is evidence of merchandise being brought from China to these countries at a very early date, and it is thought likely that the peach was introduced through this channel. There is evidence of the peach growing in Greece and Italy round about the first century A.D. It would appear that these peaches grown in far-off days were of large size, not much less than the present-day varieties. The peach was also grown in France at an early date, being mentioned in the fifth century, and doubtless had arrived in that country from

Italy. It seems to have been cultivated in this country from early times, and King John is mentioned as having eaten them. In those early days the monks in their monastery gardens practised gardening in good style, and they no doubt included peaches among the plants they grew. It seems probable they were grown as bushes, as the method of growing them trained on walls came in Elizabethan days, and this method of growing them on warm walls persisted as the sole method till fairly recent times, but attempts have been made in recent years to grow them in the open as bushes with varying degrees of success.

Peaches reproduce readily from stones; the resulting trees usually produce good fruit, and in some varieties quite a large percentage of the seedlings come true to name. This easy means of reproduction would have facilitated the spread of the peach from the one country to the other, and quite probably some found their way here during the Roman era. In the early days of peach growing in America, a very great number of trees were raised from stones and they mostly produced fine fleshy fruits. Of course, in those countries with warmer summers, the favourable states of America, Italy and Southern France and South Africa, the crop is grown entirely on bushes. An American acquaintance in the Services here during the war was amazed to see the way we grow them trained on walls, 'All this detail', he exclaimed. The peach seems to be happy growing in any country with a temperate climate, and will grow happily with any amount of heat in the summers, provided the winters are cold enough to give the trees complete rest. It has been found that in countries where they do not get this rest, the trees do not long survive in a healthy condition.

Types. There are three main groups of peaches found in China: the round peach which we favour in this country; the pointed peach not so hardy as the former. At one time France grew several varieties of the pointed type, and we see traces of this group in some of our modern varieties, and I give 'Thomas Rivers' as an example of this. However, the round peach is the one commonly grown throughout Europe today. Then there is the flat peach, somewhat like a medlar in general appearance, not grown in this country, but grown in some countries outside China.

CHAPTER ELEVEN

OUTDOOR CULTIVATION

UNDOUBTEDLY the best way to grow peaches outdoors in this country is trained on a warm brick wall. The protection the wall gives against cold winds, and the solar heat collected during the day and radiated during the night is of the greatest benefit to the trees, ensuring the ripening of the wood, which is so very necessary even in less favourable seasons. One gets a striking example of the difference between wall grown and open ground grown peaches at the East Malling Research Station. On the walls there are very good specimen trees, carrying heavy crops of fruit in most seasons, but in the open part of the same walled garden there are bush trees planted several years ago, which have by now grown into large trees, but have never given anything but a sprinkling of fruit, and some I believe have not fruited at all. There seems to be quite a lot of young wood affected with dieback to be cut out each year, some from frost damage where the wood is too soft, and some from bacterial trouble, it seems, which again attacks more readily unripened wood.

Preparation of Border or Site. If peaches are to be wall planted, either several along a run of border or at a single station on a limited wall space, it will well pay to prepare the site in the same way as advised for vines, with a similar soil mixture. If, however, the existing soil must remain this should receive a thorough preparation by bastard trenching two spits deep, and at least 3 ft. out from the wall (double or treble this width would be better). Good drainage is absolutely essential, and if there is any doubt as to the efficiency of the natural drainage, a good layer of broken bricks or tiles or clinker should be placed in the bottom as the work proceeds. This is also a good place to get rid of any old bones which may be lying around. Some good cow or horse manure may be worked into the bottom spit, provided it is put deeply enough not to come into direct contact with the roots when planting, but is put in a position where the roots can find it later on. This trenching work should be carried out several weeks before planting, to give the soil time to settle well.

Spread on the surface beforehand some lime rubble, wood or bonfire ash, and coarse bonemeal or $\frac{1}{4}$-in. bones at $\frac{1}{2}$ lb. to the square yard, and mix in well as digging proceeds. If there is difficulty in disposing of water draining from the bottom of the border owing to the lie of the land, it can sometimes be overcome by raising the level of the soil by a foot or so. It is better to do this, and lose that much height of wall, than to risk having water lying under the roots and thereby causing them to suffer from cold, wet feet, which they dislike as much as do human beings.

Planting. If the trees are being bought from a nursery-man, when they arrive, if the soil is in a fit state get them planted at once, or heel them in temporarily. If the ground is frozen hard when they arrive, keep them still in their packing, in a cold shed. Never place them in a warm shed.

If they have to be kept about for some time, make sure that the roots do not become too dry.

The ideal way is to start with a maiden tree, a tree, that is, one year after it has been budded in the nursery, but it is not often possible to obtain them at this age. When planting, take out a hole large enough to take the roots easily when they are spread straight out.

Any large roots that have been broken in the lifting should be cut off cleanly to take away the damaged root tissue. Plant at the same level as the tree was in the soil before lifting: this will usually be indicated by a mark on the stem. This should leave something like 3 in. of the stock above ground, which is very important, as the trees are grafted on this special stock, so that certain qualities of fruitfulness and control of the amount of growth the tree will make are imparted to it from the stock. If the tree is planted too deeply and the union is at or below ground level, then roots will be emitted from the scion, and the tree would probably grow away much too strongly. Plant when the soil is in the right condition, that is, when it is not too wet or frosty, and tread the soil firmly as the hole is filled in. Apply a mulch to the surface after planting, spread well in excess of the extent of the roots to conserve soil moisture, and to prevent hard frost from entering the soil, thus giving the tree a better chance to re-establish itself quickly.

Training. If starting with a maiden tree (Fig. 14), then training into a fan-shaped specimen can be carried out in what we might call the classic style. This is carried out by confining the tree to two main branches opposite each

14. *A maiden peach, one year old.*

other (Fig. 15), as near as possible developing equally, and allowing no centre growth after the first year. A maiden tree will consist of one straight stem (Fig. 14), possibly with some feathering which can be ignored and in any case will be cut away. After planting, this single growth should be cut hard back to three eyes suitably placed at a point not far above the point of union. The two bottom ones should be as near as possible opposite one another pointing outwards, and the resultant growths from these must be carefully preserved, as they will be the basis of the two main branches. The top bud should also be allowed to grow upwards, pinching out the growing point when it is about 2 ft. long, so that most of the strength is concentrated in the side growths, and they in this first year should be grown in an upwards direction. Keep them well balanced in growth, and if one is found

to be growing stronger than the other this can be recti-
fied by elevating the weaker one, and lowering the strong
one.

After the first year's growth the centre is cut out cleanly
at the fork, and the two side branches cut hard back. Two
growths from each side should be allowed to develop

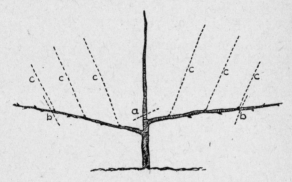

15. *A fan-trained peach two years old.* a, *central
growth cut away at one year old;* b, *prune to here in
second year;* c, *growths in third year.*

during the summer, and they in turn should be cut hard
back in the winter, and from each of these two or three
growths are taken up again (Fig. 15). This should give
about ten main branches, and the framework of a well-
balanced tree will be formed (Fig. 16). Any subsequent
development of branches will be governed by the amount
of space to be covered. The smaller fruit-producing
shoots will now be produced.

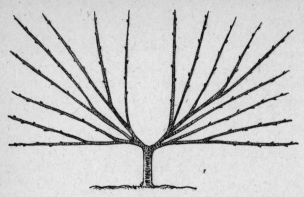

16. *Four-year-old fan-trained peach tree without central growth.*

17. *Three-year-old fan-trained peach with central growth.*

Usually the tree from the nurseryman will be from two to four years old, and the building up of the tree will be from where the nurseryman left off. It will usually be found that the tree has a centre growth, and the side branches are trained from it (Fig. 17). On trees such as this all growths should be pruned back half-way after planting to restore balance between top growth and the root system, the latter having suffered some loss in the lifting.

If there is a centre branch, this should be cut back hard to three favourably placed buds, two on opposite sides to form two more branches and the top one for a leader, and this should be repeated each year till enough branches are formed, when the centre growth should be taken out cleanly.

Managing a Fan-trained Tree. To manage a fan-trained tree as it develops in size it is essential to understand the habit of fruiting and of growth making. After the initial period of making the tree, say four or five years, and growing on a wall, the tree should start to fruit, and bear a good crop every year in increasing numbers as the tree gets larger. It is the habit of the peach to fruit on young growths made the previous season, but it will also fruit on short spurs which will be older than one year. Therefore the aim should be to see to it that each season there is a sufficiency of young growths to replace those that have carried the fruit, and this replacement growth should be taken from as near the base of the fruiting growth as is possible (Fig. 18).

18. a, *fruiting growth;* b, *fruit;* c, *successional growth.*

Disbudding. A peach tree usually makes far more growth than is needed, therefore control by disbudding has to be practised, and this consists of rubbing out unwanted growths when they are young. The aim when disbudding should be to leave a replacement shoot at the base of each fruit-bearing growth, one shoot around the middle to draw sap, and the leader, which should be left to grow on if needed for extension, but otherwise stopped when about 9 in. or 1 ft. in length. The shoot growing from the middle should also be stopped, by pinching out the growing point, when it has made about six or eight leaves. This disbudding should be carried out all over the tree, but not too much at one time. The operation should be spread

72

over a period of several days, starting with that part of the tree which is most forward. All foreright growths, that is, those growing outwards and those growing towards the wall, should be taken first, and the replacement shoot is best taken from the upper side of the fruiting growth.

Growth Buds and Flower Buds. If the leading growths or the fruiting ones are shortened at all at pruning time, then great care must be taken always to cut to a growth

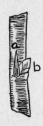

19. Left:
double bud.
a, *growth bud;*
b, *fruit bud.*
Right: *triple bud.*
a, *growth bud;*
b, *fruit buds.*

bud. Growth buds may be distinguished from flower buds quite easily: a growth bud is narrow and pointed, a flower bud is rounder and fatter and more pronounced. Sometimes the growth bud is alone, and sometimes it is the centre one of triple buds, the two outside ones being flower buds (Fig. 19). Sometimes there is one of each (Fig. 19), or sometimes a single flower bud. The short fruit spurs vary in length from 1 to 2 in. to 6 to 9 in., and usually have a cluster of flower buds at the extremity, and more flower and growth buds along their length (Fig. 20). Where flower buds are scarce on the succes-

20. *Short
fruiting spur.*
a, *growth buds;*
b, *fruit buds.*

sional growths, these fruiting spurs come in handy to fill
a gap, where otherwise fruit would be scarce.

It will be seen, when contemplating pruning or summer
management, that all growths more than one year old
comprise the main branches and the subsidiary smaller
ones, and are a permanent part of the tree, there for the
purpose of carrying the young fruiting shoots. The fruiting growths should be spaced at from 4 to 6 in. apart,
and the walls for training should be wired, if possible,
with gauge 14 galvanized wire, spaced 6 in. apart, and
about 2 or 3 in. from the wall.

The Flowering Period. The peach on a warm wall flowers
early, from the end of March onwards, and therefore it
is wise to afford some protection against frost and cold
winds. Fruit netting or heavier tennis boundary netting
is suitable, and should be hung in front of the trees during
the time they are in flower. The netting should be hung
from the top of the wall, and some bean rods or long
bamboo canes placed in a sloping position at shortish
intervals will prevent the trees from getting rubbed. By
this simple method I ensured a full crop of peaches from
twenty trees from 1938 to 1950, during which time some
winters were severe, with cold springs. This netting can

be left in position the whole time the blossom is out, and a little longer if the weather is bad, as enough light and air gets through. If something in the nature of hessian is used as curtains, they must only be fixed over the trees at night, and drawn back during the day. It is not usual at this early date for many bees to be on the wing, so it is advisable to fertilize by hand, using a rabbit's or hare's tail tied to a cane, doing it in the middle of the day on sunny occasions.

Fruit Thinning. If there is a good set, there will be very many more fruit than can be left to mature, and an early start should be made on the very necessary task of thinning. Take off first of all those towards the wall and on the under side of the shoots, as the best-quality fruits are produced where they face the sun. Then where there are clusters, reduce these to one fruit. This first thinning should be done when the little peaches are about the size of small peas and when completed left about 2 or 3 in. apart all over the tree. More can be taken off gradually as they develop, and the best-placed fruit can be spotted, until finally, that is after stoning, they should be left to mature at from 6 to 9 in. apart for the smaller varieties, and from 9 in. to 1 ft. for the larger ones. Nectarines can be left a little closer, about 6 in. apart being sufficient space for them.

Ripening. To obtain first-class quality in peaches it is imperative that the fruits obtain all the direct sun it is possible to give them, therefore, after stoning, the foliage should be fixed clear of them.

Picking. The peach fruit is produced without a stem, so

some care is needed when gathering to see that the fruit is not bruised. It is best accomplished by cupping the fingers behind the fruit and gently applying pressure.

If it is ready it will come away. For home consumption the fruit should be left to ripen thoroughly on the tree, as the flavour then is so much better. It means going over the tree daily while ripening is in progress.

Pruning. As soon as all the fruit has been gathered, prune away the growths which have borne the fruit, as this will allow more sun and air to reach the replacement growths and hasten their ripening. During the summer the young growths must be tied in loosely with raffia, so that they grow in the right direction.

During the winter any pruning which might be necessary should be done, most of the old ties cut away and the tree tied in again. During the growing season the tree's water requirements must be met, and if it is carrying a good crop of fruit some feeding must be done, applying a fruit manure such as 'Le Fruitier', or Thompson's Vine Manure, or any reliable make. A good mixture may be made at home of 2 parts of bonemeal, 2 parts of hoof and horn, and 1 part of sulphate of potash.

Apply this at 4 oz. to the square yard, and water it in well. Liquid manure made from animal droppings is also good.

Reinvigorating Trees. There comes a time when peach and nectarine trees get old and weak and need reinvigorating. They cannot be cut hard back into old wood, as can apples and pears, but they can often be restored to health by removing the top two or three inches of the old soil over the root area, giving a dressing of manure as above, and top dressing with either turfy loam rotted down, or good soil from a vegetable plot, adding a good proportion of mortar rubble. Also cut hard back about half the young growths.

THE PEACH GROWN AS A BUSH

Where the grower does not happen to have a suitable warm wall or the necessary time to spend on the care of a trained tree, this form of culture does offer the keen garden owner a possible chance to grow his own peaches. I think it is generally conceded that nectarines are not successful grown in this way. The management of peaches grown in bush form is comparatively simple, compared with trained trees, which should be an advantage to the inexperienced.

Building up the Tree. Building up of the tree is on similar lines to those adopted for apples. If you are starting with a maiden, cut back to within about 1 ft. of the ground, taking up three or four of the resulting growths as a start to the framework. By cutting back the leaders fairly hard for the next two years, a good framework of main branches will be built up (Fig. 21).

After this the young fruiting wood may be allowed to develop naturally, doing no disbudding of the growths. Pruning should be confined to the cutting out of dead wood, and removing surplus and crossing branches in May. An American variety, Rochester, is very good for growing in this form, as is also the variety Peregrine.

21. *A bush peach.*

STOCKS FOR BUDDING

Although peaches will grow quite well budded on to their own stocks raised from stones, it is not often done in this country. For fan-trained trees which are not required to grow too large, the Mussel stock (which is a type of plum) is usually preferred. If a larger tree is required, then the stronger growing Brompton stock is used.

If anyone desires to try budding peaches on stocks

78

raised from peach stones, as there can be no growth unless the stone is cracked and the kernel freed, the stones should be kept in moist soil through the winter, and in early March carefully cracked and planted out of doors in sandy soil. Some might be ready for budding by late summer when budding is done. Grafting is not usually resorted to, as it is often unsuccessful owing to gumming.

PESTS AND DISEASES

Peaches outdoors, if properly looked after, are not attacked by many pests. A routine winter spray of tar-oil wash will usually keep them clear of aphis, at least for some months. If an attack comes later in the summer, spray with nicotine or other suitable insecticide. Red spider can be troublesome in a hot season, and plenty of spraying of the foliage with clear water in the evenings is the best answer to this. Ants are sometimes troublesome on the ripe fruit, but DDT spread round the stem of the tree will deal with them. Mussel scale is not much seen now, and a winter wash of tar oil or DNC petroleum gives complete control.

Peach Leaf Curl. This is a fungus disease which attacks peaches out of doors. Trees under glass are never troubled with it. The disease produces much curled leaves with thickened tissue. The leaves turn red and eventually drop off. The trouble can be controlled by spraying in early spring, at the end of February, with lime sulphur at 1 part to 30 of water, or a copper wash such as Bouisol,.

can be used if preferred. This should be an annual routine job.

Trees sometimes suffer from die back. The remedy is to cut out the infected wood, back to sound growth, and spray with Bouisol at the recommended strength.

CHAPTER TWELVE

CULTIVATION UNDER GLASS

In many respects culture under glass will follow the same pattern as that of growing trained trees on walls outside. When choosing a tree for a specific situation in a house, it does often occur that a certain length of stem is required, sometimes up to as long as 3 ft. for the purpose of bringing the branches up into the light.

Border Construction. If a border is to be constructed, it should be on very much the same lines as recommended for grapes. The peach, however, is not quite as exacting as the vine in the matter of soil, and whereas if at all possible new turfy loam should be used for a vine border, the peach will be quite happy if some old potting soil or even some good soil from a vegetable plot is mixed in, even up to half the bulk. It is not advisable to have the soil too good for young peaches or they may make too vigorous growth, which will be unfruitful, and necessitate root pruning, a laborious and lengthy operation which no one wants to be burdened with under present-day conditions.

Training. If certain growths on a young tree tend to grow away too strongly, the trouble can be partly if not completely overcome by depressing these strong growths and tying them in this position, and if any of the main growths show signs of growing weakly, they should be brought into a more upright position. In the initial training of young trees, bamboo canes should be used in conjunction with the wires on which to train the growths.

Forcing. With the use of glasshouses, the season of ripe fruit can be much extended. With the necessary degree of heat at hand, the earliest fruits may be gathered in May, from suitable early varieties such as James Walker, Duke of York and Waterloo. For this earliest forcing, a start has to be made as early as November; at first incitement to growth must be very gradual, using no fire heat, merely closing the house at nights. After about three weeks, a little fire heat may be introduced, gradually increasing the temperature to 45° at night, 50° in the day-time. It should be somewhere around this at flowering time, a little less rather than more. After setting, and when the fruit is about the size of peas, then the heat must be raised quite considerably to 60° at night and 70° in the day-time. As the trees will be doing everything that much earlier, they should be rested earlier, keeping full air on the house after the fruit has been gathered. Growing in pots is probably the best way to grow very early peaches, as the trees then can be stood outside after fruiting, where ripening of the wood will be much more complete. But to most this very early forcing will now be only a memory or a dream, and ripe fruit towards the end of June and on through the summer months will more likely be the order of things, with the latest varieties ripening in cold houses at the end of September and October. This will call for little or no fire heat. To obtain ripe fruit in June and early July calls for a little in the early stages, otherwise cold houses will supply all the protection needed. Peaches and nectarines, generally speaking, need much less heat than grapes, and are better off with more air at all times. I think I should mention here that the nectarines best suited for early forcing are Cardinal, Early Rivers and Lord Napier.

ROUTINE MANAGEMENT

The successful cultivation of peaches under glass calls for more routine work than when they are growing in the open, in that they have to be syringed regularly (or, later in the season, when the foliage has toughened up a bit, spraying with the hose may be brought into operation) to keep pests, especially red spider, in check.

Starting into Growth. When the trees are started early in the season, the trees should be sprayed early in the day with tepid water. The spraying is done early so that the trees are dry before nightfall, when the temperature will be fairly low, and on dull days the spraying should be omitted altogether. Floors and all bare spaces should be damped down, more or less according to outside conditions. A little air should be admitted during the day whenever possible, the amount to be governed by outside conditions. During the spell of arctic weather in February 1956, when we had hard frost at night, and several degrees of frost persisted in the day-time, and when it was very difficult to get any air on even during the day, our trees were in full bloom. We managed to keep the temperature at about 38° F. at night, which is safe. Actual frost must be kept from the flowers, apart from this they will stand a fairly low temperature. Too much fire heat is much

more likely to do them harm, and prevent them setting.
The Flowering Period. At the time the trees are in bloom
it is usual to stop syringeing, to ensure the pollen being
perfectly dry by midday and in the correct condition for
fertilization to be carried out successfully.

It is not wise to keep the house too dry, and damping
down may be carried out each day after pollination has
been done. Some growers are of the opinion that a light
misting of the blooms with tepid water is an aid to setting;
this again should be done early, so that the pollen may dry
by midday. The use of the rabbit's tail and disbudding
and fruit thinning must all be carried out as advised for
outside management. As soon as the blossoming period
is past, syringeing and normal damping down must be
resumed.

Spring and Summer Routine. Towards the end of April
it might well become advisable to give a second light
syringeing just after midday, during very warm weather;
but the trees must not be wet at night this early in the
season. Later on, in high summer when nights are very
warm, from June onwards, it is often desirable to have
moisture on the foliage during the night, and therefore
during fine spells syringeing should be done in the evening, but not during cool, wet spells: the trees will be
healthier if kept dry overnight when these latter conditions prevail. During May and June tying in of the young
growths must be attended to, as the initial part of their
training, and also to let sun and light to the fruit.

Damping down will need to be done oftener during

summer, morning, midday and evening during warm spells.

Feeding. Trees that are carrying full crops of fruit will need some assistance, and should be fed with a good fruit-tree manure after thinning the fruit, and again after the stoning period. A mulch of stable manure may be applied about March or April, and this will especially benefit old trees. Occasional applications of weak liquid manure will be of the greatest benefit. Great care must always be exercised in the feeding of young trees, for if it is over-done rank growths will result, the balance of the tree will be upset, and it will take a long time to put things right. The trees must never be allowed to get dry at the roots, and watering of the border, when done, must be done thoroughly.

Shading. In some houses, and this applies especially to lean-to houses facing south, some light shading will need to be given the trees from May onwards. The easiest way is to spray it on to the roof glass, using a solution of green-house shading or ordinary distemper in white or green. Nectarines are much more susceptible to scorching of the fruit than is the peach, probably because they have smooth skins.

The downy skin of the peach does, no doubt, protect it to a certain extent. There is no hard-and-fast rule on this matter of shading, the decision must be made on each house as it stands, as so much depends upon the aspect and orientation, and most of all on the angle of the roof. Scorching is much more likely to occur in a house with a sharply rising roof than it is where the roof is set at a more flattened angle.

Ripening. A the fruits approach the ripening stage, afford them all the sun and light possible, by tying back any foliage which overhangs them. They may be brought more up to the light by fixing a large wooden label at the back of the fruit, and in turn fixing the label to the wires. As the fruits begin to ripen on a tree, all syringeing of that particular tree must cease, until all the fruit has been gathered, when syringeing or hosing must be resumed with as much force as can be used without damaging the foliage. As much air as possible must be admitted at all times now, to aid in the ripening of the young wood.

Pruning. Pruning may be done at any time after the picking of the fruit up till the time the trees are tied in anew.

Cleaning. In the late autumn, and for preference before the end of the year, cut all the old ties, bunch the branches into convenient-sized lots and tie them temporarily to the wires; thoroughly wash the inside of the house with hot soapy water, with a dash of nicotine mixed in, and wash down with clean water, with plenty of force. Give the trees a spraying with tar-oil wash at 4 per cent strength, provided it is done before the end of December; it is not safe to use it later than this.

Tying In. The tree must be then tied in again, using tarred string for the larger branches and raffia for the fruiting wood. To get a good finished article, each branch and subsidiary branch should be tied as straight as possible, from their source, to either their extremity, or to where they fork. No wood should be allowed to cross, but young wood may be tied along bare old wood for coverage.

Overhauling the Border. This completed, the border should receive its annual overhaul, lightly pricking and taking off the top inch or two of the old soil, and replacing with new rotted loam, to each barrowload of which has been added a 6-in. potful of bonemeal and a 4-in. potful of sulphate of potash.

ON OTHER OCCUPANTS OF THE FRUIT HOUSES

It often happens that other plants are accommodated in vineries and peach houses, but where this is so, the good of the vines and trees should always come first, and care should be taken to allow in only those plants which will not interfere with the well-being of the main occupants.

CHAPTER THIRTEEN

VARIETIES OF PEACHES
AND NECTARINES

VARIETIES OF PEACHES

THE varieties of peaches we grow in this country are mostly of the round type, with a soft and very juicy melting flesh, mostly pale in colour, whitish or whitish green, sometimes with crimson colouring next the stone, or in some a yellowish white. Practically all are free stone, that is, the flesh parts readily from the stone. All varieties except the latest are suitable for growing under glass, or outdoors on warm walls in the south, but in the north and in Scotland only the early varieties are suitable for growing outdoors. For most of the best of our present-day varieties we owe a great deal of gratitude to Thomas Rivers, the famous nurseryman of Sawbridgeworth, and his successors. He raised and sent out most of them in the latter half of the last century. America also made a notable contribution in sending the varieties, Amsden June, Hale's Early and Waterloo, all early varieties of medium size, ripening some days before anything else we have. The identification of peaches and nectarines should be fairly easy, as in addition to the fruit, which admittedly is not always easy to identify a variety by, we have large and small flowers, and a distinctive foliage character in the form of glands on the stem at the base of the leaves, and they vary, in that some are round some kidney shape, and in some varieties they are absent. Even so, much care is needed by the nurseryman to keep stocks true.

Alexander. One of the early varieties from America, ripens outside on a south wall towards the end of July. Fruit fairly large, dark red on exposed side, juicy and of good flavour. Flowers large.

Alexandra Noblesse (Rivers). One of the very best, and excellent for a cold house. Fruit very large, pale yellow in colour, with a few red dots on the sunny side. Flesh fairly firm, pale yellow, melting, very rich, of nectarine-like quality. Ripens mid-August. Flowers large.

Barrington. Fruit large, flesh greenish-white, rich and of first-class flavour. Skin downy, pale greenish, dark red on exposed side. Strong grower. Ripens mid-September. Flowers large.

Bellegarde. Of French origin. Fruit large, crimson streaked with crimson purple. Flesh pale yellow, of first-class quality, very rich and melting. Red round the stone. Ripens mid-September. Flowers small.

Crimson Galande (Rivers). Fruit medium, somewhat flattened. Skin thin, speckled with red, dark red on exposed side. Flesh of first-rate quality, red next to the stone. Tree of strong constitution. Late August. Flowers small.

Dymond. Fruit very large, palish yellow, red dots and bright red on exposed side. White flesh, melting, sweet, of good flavour. Strong grower and good cropper. Excellent for exhibition. Mid-August. Flowers small.

Golden Eagle (Rivers). One of the golden fleshed late

varieties. Fruit very large, deep golden yellow, with red on exposed side. Flesh deep yellow, juicy of moderate flavour. Good for exhibition. Early October. Flowers small.

Goshawk (Rivers). Fruit large, greenish striped and flushed dull red. White flesh of exceptionally good quality. Early September, flowers large.

Hale's Early. An early variety. Fruit medium large, greenish flushed dark red. Flesh white, juicy, of moderately good quality. End of July. Flowers large.

Nectarine Peach. Fruit very large, greenish yellow, some red on exposed side. Flesh white, tender and juicy of moderate flavour. Late September. Flowers large.

Peregrine (Rivers). Probably the best all round peach, doing well inside or out. If only one is grown, this is the one. Fruit is large, with brilliant dark red colouring, practically all over. Flesh firm, rich and of excellent flavour. Early to mid-August. Flowers large.

Prince of Wales. Fruit large, green with bright red. Flesh melting, of good flavour. Crops abundantly. Mid-September. Flowers small.

Princess of Wales (Rivers). Fruit very large, cream colour, with rose on exposed side. Flesh melting, juicy and excellent. Good for exhibition. Early October. Flowers large.

Rochester. An American variety, which finds favour with the bush-peach enthusiasts. Fruit of medium size, of good quality. Mid-August.

Salwey. A late golden-fleshed variety. Raised by Colonel Salwey in 1850 from the stone of an Italian peach. Flesh soft, moderate quality. Best suited for a cold house. Flowers small. Early October.

Sea Eagle (Rivers). Fruit very large, more elongated than most, greenish yellow, red on the exposed side. Flesh white, soft, moderately good flavour. Good for cold house, or south wall outside. Late September. Flowers large.

Thomas Rivers. Very large. Pale yellow, with light red flush. Fruit pointed, flesh soft, moderate quality. End September. Flowers large.

Walburton Admirable. Fruit very large. Yellowish green, with crimson and darker mottlings on the exposed side. Flesh melting, rich and of very good flavour. Robust grower and fruitful. End of September. Flowers small.

Waterloo. One of the early American varieties. Fruit medium, flattened, crimson nearly all over. Melting, juicy, and of good flavour. Mid-July. Flowers large.

VARIETIES OF NECTARINES

Cardinal (Rivers). Fruit medium, pale green, bright red on the exposed side. One of the earliest, suitable for a warm house. Good flavour. Early July. Flowers large.

Dryden. Fruit very large, green with red dots, and dark red on exposed side. Flesh melting, sweet and of good flavour. End of August. Flowers small.

Early Rivers. Fruit large, greenish white, bright red on exposed side. Flesh white, melting, excellent flavour. Similar to Lord Napier, but earlier. End of July. Flowers large.

Elruge. Fruit medium, pale green, dark red next the sun.

Flesh white, melting, delicious flavour. A good grower and crops well. End of August. Flowers small.

Humboldt (Rivers). Fruit large, yellow, dark red where best. Mid-August. Flowers large and decorative.

Lord Napier (Rivers). Fruit large, pale green, with bright red where exposed. Flesh white, juicy and very rich. One of the best in the white-fleshed varieties. Mid-August. Flowers large.

John Rivers. Fruit large, palish green with red. Of excellent flavour. Mid-July. Flowers large.

Pineapple (Rivers). Similar to Humboldt, but not so deep in colour. Fruit large, golden yellow, with a little red. Flesh juicy, sweet, and of excellent pineapple flavour. An excellent variety. Early September. Flowers large.

Spenser. Fruit very large, greenish, very dark dull red where exposed. Flesh white and melting. Flavour good. Splendid for exhibition. Mid-September. Flowers large.

Stanwick Elruge (Rivers). An improvement on the old Elruge, superior to it in size and colour.

Victoria. One of the best flavoured of the late varieties. Greenish, with dull dark red. Medium size. Mid-September. Flowers small.